Stop! Stop!!
MAKING
BAD
DESIGN

The accelerated guide
to better design
and lifestyle for
Graphic designers
and creatives

ESEKWE VICTOR

Stop! Stop!!
Making Bad Design

The accelerated guide to better design and lifestyle for Graphic designers and creatives.

Esekwe Victor

Copyright

TABLE OF CONTENTS

Dedication

This book is dedicated to thousands of creative people whose craft are often undervalued and unappreciated, yet still, strive to produce the best work they can. They are the real MVPs.

Introduction

This book is short and super concise, yet has the potential to give you a comprehensive foundation on most topics regarding graphic design, as well as practical guides anyone needs to start out as a graphic designer. And if you are already practicing, with little experience, this book is still relevant to you, as it can enhance the quality of your work, in ways that you've least expected.

Also, if you're looking for ways to improve the visual appeal of your social media posts, then this book is for you. Contained in it are principles that can be applied to a broad range of areas.

Cheers! Let's get started.

Introduction to Graphic Design

According to Wikipedia, graphic design is the process of visual communication and problem-solving through the use of typography (text), photography (images), iconography, and illustration (lines, shapes, color etc.).

In a nutshell, graphic design is using graphical elements such as text, lines, color, shapes, images, etc., to communicate a story or idea clearly and aesthetically (pleasing to the eye).

Graphic design is broad in scope and finds application in various areas such as; branding (logo design and brand identity), product packaging design, web design, signage, digital illustration, UI/UX, animation/motion graphics, and the list goes on and on.

The building blocks of every graphic design are;

- LINES

A line is formed when a movement is made from one point to another on a given space. Lines define boundaries and are very basic but powerful.

Lines come in variety of forms; thin, thick, straight, curved, zigzag etc.

- SHAPES

When the boundaries of an object are close, then you have a shape. Shapes come in varying forms, such as circles, triangles, squares, hexagons, etc. There are organic and geometric shapes. Organic shapes are loosely defined and have boundaries that cannot be constructed using laws of geometry. Geometric shapes, on the other hand, are well defined and obey the laws of geometry.

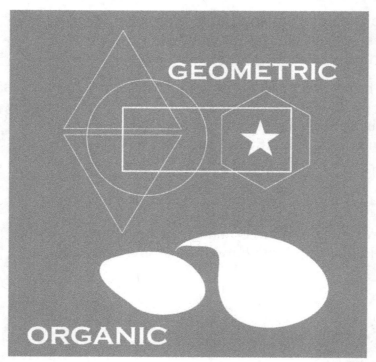

- TYPOGRAPHY

Typography is the art of lettering; it is the design of glyphs (letterforms, punctuations) that enables the designer to pass across a message. Typefaces are grouped into various categories that will be discussed more in a specialized chapter.

- COLOUR

Colour is the property reflected by a substance when it is hit by light. It is usually measured in terms of hue (another word for colour), saturation (intensity), brightness, etc. There is a whole chapter dedicated to colour.

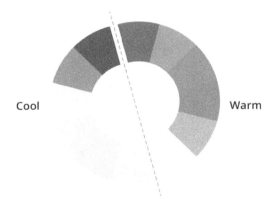

Image credit: Pinterest.com

- TEXTURE

This refers to the smoothness or roughness of a surface. Texture in a design is necessary as it can add a lot of difference to how a design feels and what it communicates.

- VALUE

Value refers to the lightness or darkness of a design. Irrespective of colour, there are light and dark shades of every colour that are defined by the saturation.

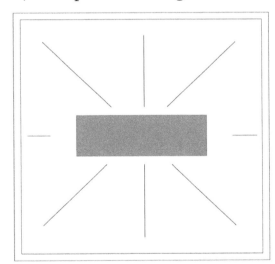

- SPACE

Space is the empty area around design element, often designated as negative space. It is an "enemy" to amateurs as they want to get rid of it, but experienced designers use it to their advantage.

- SIZE

Size refers to the magnitude of elements. It is necessary for balance, a line for instance can be made thin or thick. A shape can be increased or reduced. An image can be magnified or reduced. All must be done

6

with the aim of getting a well-rounded design. Balanced is discussed further under design theory.

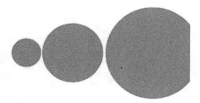

Other important elements include Images. And they must be selected with great care. Copyright issues must be resolved, even as appropriate images are used to covey central information.

Also, the image quality must be great. Images are of two kinds; Bitmap and vector. Bitmap is stored in pixels and include our normal image formats such as .jpg, .jpeg, .png etc.

On the other hand, Vector images are stored as mathematical equations and must be read by specific software. This category of images can be scaled to any size without image quality reduction. But the same cannot be said for bitmap.

When you work on a design software, the artwork is usually stored in vector form. But when exported, it becomes a bitmap file that can be read by any image viewing software on any device.

An image of poor resolution will cause a bad design. So make sure you get high-quality stock images and resize to your taste. This is better than downloading a poor resolution image and trying to scale it up, which usually leads to blurred images most times.

Your ability to combine elements, using the appropriate software and design knowledge to communicate an idea, story, etc. is what makes you a good graphic designer. A bad designer is one who fails to appreciate the importance of little things. He or she takes theory unserious, and refuses to take correction on critiqued work.

Pretty straightforward, right?

But trust me; there is a whole lot to learn. The learning curve is steep. But dedicating hours to practice is the best way to learn. You can view the works of others and take mental notes. Also, reading books (such as this), watching videos, and keeping up with design trends are practical actions you don't want to treat with negligence.

Frankly speaking, a lot of things go into becoming a professional. But then, don't get overwhelmed or tired in the process. Practice makes perfection!

Now let us see two examples of these blocks in action.

Problem 1: I want to pass across a message that "talent is never enough and hard work is needed."

Now see as this graphic design is broken down into its most basic element.

Shapes: The design is enclosed in a square dimensioned shape.

Lines: We see zigzag lines and thin lines coming from the top and bottom.

Typography: Here we see texts with their various fonts and colors.

Colors: The background is ___ the texts have their colors ___ image has a kind of coloration too. All colors have been chosen expertly.

Image: A ballerina dancing has been chosen which depicts the idea being passed across.

Problem2: I want to pass across a message that "Exclusive breastfeeding for the first six months is important."

Now see as this graphic design is broken down into its most basic elements.

Shapes: Here we see a rectangle filled with yellow color to create some highlight.

Lines: This logo here has some lines, very small but if you look well there are curves joined together.

Typography: Two fonts and colors have been used for the texts.

Images: This design has the image as the main focus, so two images of women breastfeeding "obvious" to our message have been chosen and expertly blended to look like one.

Knowing that every design can be s... reduce the anxiety associated with learning to improve your graphic designs.

What software(s) do I learn

Of course there is always the question of what software to learn.

Before attempting to learn the use of certain software, I always advise people to learn the basics first (that's design theory), which I'll talk about in the next chapter.

The reason is simple; you must know how to craft a design without any software i.e. in your mind, using pen and paper before you can bring it to life with any chosen software. So don't be in a hurry to get fancy software yet.

If you don't know your onions, be patient to learn... and as you learn, then you get appropriate software to practice depending on your main field of specialization.

Adobe products have become the industry standard (they are not free). Photoshop and illustrator are a must; CorelDraw is also a great substitute for illustrator. There are numerous softwares and covering them all is almost impossible.

However, if you are into motion graphics and animation then software like adobe after effects, davinci resolve, blender, etc. will be very useful for you. But for a start, Adobe Illustrator, Photoshop, and/or CorelDraw will do just fine to create all of the designs I will be showing you in this book.

As you progress, you will discover that you don't need to know how to use a lot of software but know how to use a few very well. So pick the software, check the interface and see if you are comfortable with it.

All that being said, cost also factors in this selection process. So consider all that and make your pick. Some free graphic design software include Canva,Gravit designer, inkscape, Pixlr, etc.

So once you get the software, the next thing is to know how to use the basic tool. Don't be in a hurry because it takes a lot of dedication (perhaps years) to become an expert in any software. Thereafter, watch tutorials on it, reproduce a lot of works and give yourself mini-projects.

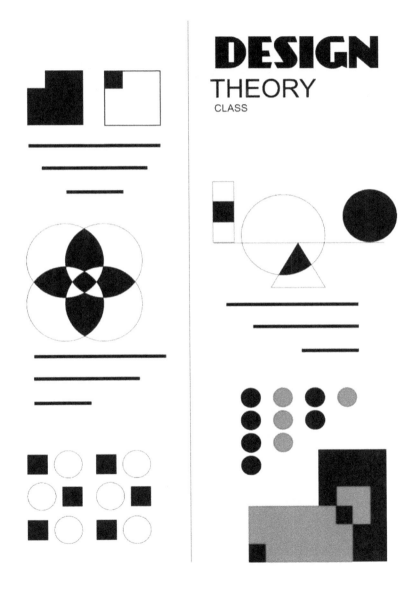

There are many theories which guide functional, creative design. These rules are not a means to stifle expression but a guide to make you create standard work, which can compete with the best anywhere in the world. Here are some of the theories of design, in no particular order and brief explanations.

1. Visual Hierarchy

Visual hierarchy involves using size, weight, colour, boldness, etc. to give focus to the most important information in a design. For instance, the most relevant information can be made bolder, and sub-headers (less relevant ones) are given less weight and size. It is used to give design structure and direct readers to the most important information on the work. Works with a lack of hierarchy will leave readers confused and lacks proper structure.

THEN READ THIS FINALLY

READ THIS FIRST

THEN READ THIS

Your eyes (and attention) in the example above has been expertly directed using the law of visual hierarchy. Remember, one main message (boldest) and sub headers with decreased weight and size.

2. Alignment

Alignment is how graphic elements are arranged or grouped together. Alignment is necessary to create visual appeal. A disorganized work is an eyesore and this is a mistake rookies make. There are three types of alignment; left, right and center.

Here these three lines have been aligned to the left, center and right. Text, shapes, lines etc. can all be aligned using rulers or grids in your preferred software.

3. Contrast

Contrast is the use of opposite design elements to create effect. It is used most especially with colours to improve readability and improve visual coherence. For instance, a dark colour on a dark background is not a good contrast. But if a dark colour is placed on a light background, it provides good contrast which is necessary for readability and aesthetic appeal.

4. Balance

Balance is the distribution of elements around your workspace. It's divided into symmetrical and asymmetrical. "Symmetrical" means that if a line divides your workspace into two halves, then these elements are divided equally among those two halves. "Asymmetrical" does not divide elements equally but uses other concepts such as weight, color, amongst others, to still create balance.

This design is asymmetric, because the Dog's head is towards one end of the page; giving that side more weight. But a text has been added with some lines to counter that, giving it balance. It's just like creating balance on a weight scale.

This work on the other hand is perfectly symmetrical. Everything has been distributed accordingly on both sides of the work.

5. Negative space/Gestalt

Negative space is the "empty space" surrounding the graphic elements in your workspace. Amateurs ignore it. But experts use it to give their work stunning effect and simplicity. Gestalt principle states that the whole is greater than the sum of its parts and it uses the ability of the human mind to fill up void spaces to create stunning designs.

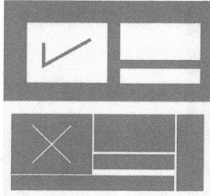

Let your design breathe, set up appropriate grids and be generous with your margins. Do not crowd your work with irrelevant information. If the information is much, then use proper hierarchy to ensure it doesn't become an eyesore.

In the first half, is there an "LS" or just spaces in the circle? In the second half, is there a triangle or just spaces in between the circles? The whole is greater than the sum of the parts.

6. Repetition

Repetition is the process of creating patterns by repeating elements in a defined manner. It works alongside another concept of proximity, which utilizes the mind's ability to see grouped objects as one.

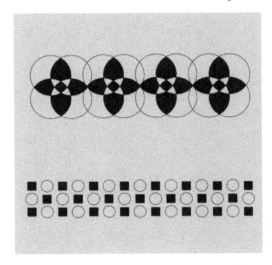

Motifs are a brilliant example of how repetition can be used to create stunning effects. Colors can also be repeated to create visual coherence

Here repetition of a colour (peach) has been used to improve the visual appeal of this work. It also draws your attention to important details.

Other theories include typography and colour theory. But these will be covered in chapters dedicated for each of them.

As you work more you will appreciate the value of these principles even more.

Working with colour

Why Colours?

Imagine creation In greyscale. The trees a dull grey, the butterflies Pitch black, the sun a white blanket... It already sounds like the intro to a very depressing scene. So colours are the spice of nature. They bring life and emotion to a work of art.

Colours evoke imagination, intrigue, and spark our enthusiasm. So much that the term "adding colour" has become synonymous with making an event, speech, or any program much more entertaining and enjoyable. So colours are a must for any person who wants to deliver graphics that work.

Colour Schemes

Colours are the reflection produced when light strikes an object. Another word for colour is "Hue," while "saturation" is the shade of that colour. For instance, blue has different saturations; one of which is navy blue.

We have primary, secondary, and tertiary colours. We also have warm, cool, and neutral colours in groups.

Primary colours are yellow, blue and red. Secondary colours are green, orange, and purple. Tertiary colours include red-violet, blue-green, yellow-orange, etc., and all the tons of shades in between. Cool colours are colours that lie on the left half of the colour wheel, while warm colours lie on the right. They are called warm because of their brightness, and the cool colours are called so because of their calm appearance.

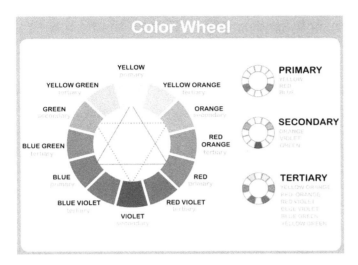

Image credit: Pinterest.com

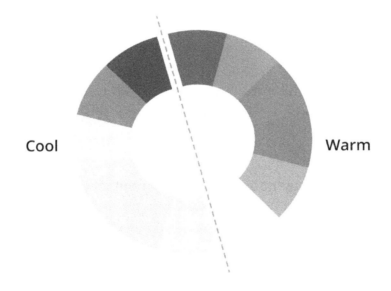

Image credit: Pinterest.com

There are three major colour models; CMYK, RGB, and Pantone. They are different in their definition of colour and associated colour codes. CMYK is used when work is to be printed as most printers use CMYK inks. RGB, Son the other hand, is used for Digital display downloads.

Work done in RGB will usually be converted to CMYK before it is taken for printing.

There are many ways for combining colours on the colour wheel and they are;

1. Monochromatic

Here, one colour is used throughout with different shades being adopted to increase effect.

2. Complementary

In this case, colours on the opposite side of the colour wheel are used, with a colour being dominant and the other recessive.

3. Analogous

Here, colours close to each other on the colour wheel are used together.

4. Triadic

This is when three colours, evenly spaced on the colour wheel are used. And usually, there is a dominant colour with the others being recessive.

5. Rectangle

It uses two complementary sets each. Care must be taken to handle it to avoid too much colours clashing.

6. Square

This is similar to the triadic but makes use of four colours, all evenly spaced.

7. Split-complementary

This is a variant of the complementary. It uses the two colours adjacent to a complementary colour on the wheel alongside that colour.

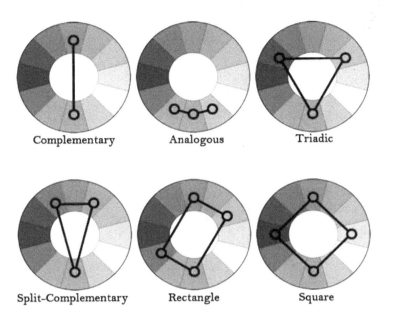

Complementary	Analogous	Triadic
Split-Complementary	Rectangle	Square

The art of mixing colours must be refined. Often times you develop a feel for picking colours after working on them for a while.

Having said all of this, I have by no means exhausted the information available on colour schemes and the technicalities of colour modes; however, the piece of information above is solid and can instantly impacts your work positively.

Using Palettes

Picking colours can be daunting for a new or even professional designer. Indeed there are tons of materials that explain colour theory, but I will give you practical shortcuts that can accelerate any project. A palette solves the problem. It is basically a group of colours that work together and creates visual harmony when paired alongside each other.

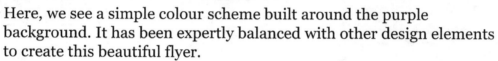

Here, we see a simple colour scheme built around the purple background. It has been expertly balanced with other design elements to create this beautiful flyer.

This is a more elaborate colour scheme. Again, we see that "balance" creates visual harmony and aesthetic appeal.

It is great to pour hours into the study of colour theory but it sure helps to download pallets related to the work being done and work with that. Using your eyedropper and fill tool, you can then apply those colours to your work. Sometimes, the client specifies a particular colour, and you just need to find schemes that work with that colour.

Even if you use a single coulour scheme, it can still be arranged properly to create solid visual effect.

In the flyer above, the main colour is orange and the other colours have been chosen to work around that colour. Yet again, the concept of balance cannot be overemphasized.

Meanwhile, it is important you research the meaning of colour in the culture of your client, the brand's objectives and intended reach. All these put together can also influence your colour choice(s) for the job at hand.

Red– Fiery, Energy, Heat, Passion, Romance, Danger, etc.

Green – Natural, growth, earthly etc.

Blue – Reliability, traditional, loyalty etc.

Pink – Feminine, Welcoming, Calm

Gold – Luxury, premium, wealth, extravagance etc.

– Purity, Calmness, Serenity etc.

A quick internet search on color psychology will give a lot of reading materials on the strategies used by brands to encourage sales and drive profits.

What is the first thing that comes to mind seeing this juice product package? I am sure it will be; healthy, natural, etc.

Well, those colours have been chosen to reflect these (some of what you have popped up in your mind). Of course, however, these colours will be inappropriate for an energy drink.

Like I said earlier, one sure way to choose appropriate colours is to get the central message of the brand or product; research the cultural environment, and then choose colour(s) that match. This is to allow you create a pallet that is visually harmonious.

Interestingly, the internet makes that job much easier for you. And also, many software have inbuilt palettes that help you make colour matching a breeze in the park.

Using too many colours is a sure way to get stuck. The trick is one primary colour and two or three secondary colours. You can add to it as many tertiary colours as you want as long as you maintain order. Primary colour here means the most dominant.

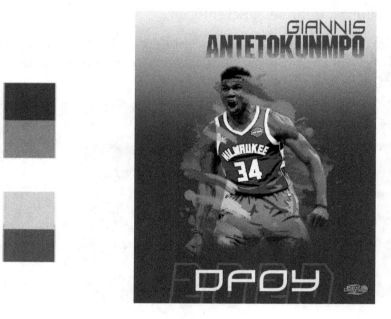

In this poster, the primary or dominant colour is green which matches the jersey colour. Note, a gradient has been applied on the background which goes from white at the top to deep green at the bottom. The secondary colours used are blue and orange, which have been applied minimally. As you can see balance has been maintained to ensure harmony.

Nonetheless, make sure you don't overdo colour selection.

Above all, continue to practice till your sense of colour combination gets better.

A typeface is a collection of alphabets, numerals, and punctuations that share a common design. There are tens of thousands of typefaces that have been created since the origin of print. A font is a sub-set of a typeface that differs from other fonts in that family in some minor details but has a wholly similar design. For instance, the Georgia typeface has font 12, which is a bit different from font 14but they are still members of the Georgia typeface.

"Type" is the most telling feature of the design. It is perhaps the soul of design because it relays information about the design purpose. Therefore it has to be gotten right. There are five classes of typeface, and we will look at them shortly;

1. Serif

They are characterized by slight extensions on the end of their strokes. Examples include; Bodoni, Cambria, Times New Roman, Rockwell, Trajan Pro, Garamond, etc. Typically, they are used for headers and copy.

2. Sans Serif

Sans Serifs are characterized by no extensions on the end of their strokes. Examples include; Impact, futura Md, Verdana, Neuropolitical, century gothic, Calibri etc. They are used for headers, copy and are usually used for website designs due to their fresh, clean look.

3. Script/Decorative

They are characterized by seamless, calligraphic styled strokes that mimic cursive handwriting, calligraphy, and other forms of penmanship. Examples include; Old English text mt, bush script mt, matura mt script, Vivaldi, freehand bj, etc. They are used for headers, subtitles but are not suitable for copy due to their readability issues.

4. Display

Display fonts vary widely in appearance. They have different styles and are useful for headers, and subtitles etc., but are not suitable for copy due to their eccentric nature. Examples include; stuntman condensed, borg, newsflash BB, Canterbury, cooper, Lane upper, Gunship condensed etc.

5. Monospaced

These are characterized by equal spacing (horizontal) by each letter. They can be serif or sans serif. They can be used for headers and copy. Examples include; courier new, lucida console, autobahn, unispace, iper.

Combining Typefaces

If you have ever undertaken any design project, you should know that combining typefaces is a daunting task. There are tons of typefaces on the market. And I do have over ten thousand typefaces installed on my computer.

Yes, the number I use actively is less than a hundred.

Combining typefaces revolve around choosing a category for the header and another for the copy. A third can be used for highlights or sub-headers. Generally, to use more than three typefaces for any job can result in disorganized work.

Two different typefaces or two variants of a particular typeface (i.e. bold and light variant) can be used.

www.fontpair.co is a great place to accelerate your project speed by checking out great font pairs, and then download them straight to your device. The list of font pairing is exhaustive, but I will not even attempt to start listing them.

For your next project, play around with combinations or check online for font pairs that work together.

Do's and Don'ts of typeface usage

There are many rules surrounding the usage of "Type" and I will list some of the major ones which must be adhered to, or not (yeah!)

1. Don't use too many typefaces for a project. There is no limit; but three is alright as a limit. More than three will require expertise in usage.
2. Resize text using the four edges, not the top and bottom. Improper resizing will distort the letterforms and ruin your work. The same applies to images.
3. Don't use too much text. Use as little text as possible, especially when designing for adverts or social media usage, unless you want to edit a book.
4. Do use legible text. Fancy typefaces are beautiful but are hardly readable. So, ensure your copy and use "headers" that are very legible. No one will stress themselves trying to understand what your "letterforms" mean.

5. Don't use inappropriate *contrast*. I talked about the contrast in the second chapter. Make sure your text contrast is visible enough; it is necessary to ensure it is readable.
6. Do ensure grammatical accuracy. Oftentimes, many designers misspell words or used poor grammar, leaving doubt in the clients about their skillfulness.
   As a professional, you are to proofread before you present your final design. Remember, the design must communicate something relevant.
7. Don't neglect *visual hierarchy*. Visual hierarchy is a no-brainer when it comes to arranging your text well and orderly. So observe it.
8. Do use alignment and grids. Alignment ensures texts are well arranged
9. Grids ensure there are proper spacing and generous margins. Their usage brings a whole new level of professionalism to your work. Negative space is your friend; make sure your work can breathe.

A great article on typeface can be found on www.toptal.com. Unless you are, or plan to be a typography designer; you might not need to know the nitty-gritty of type design.

From Briefing to Presentation

Image Credit: Pexels.com

The road from briefing to presentation is not a straight one, but there are major stops along the way that will help us simplify our projects. The major stops are explained here with examples and practical guides on making the journey easier. Let us explore...

1. Briefing

Briefing is always the first stage of a design project. It is the time where you want to take as much information as possible; depending on the project(s) involved. You should try to ask significant questions. Some things to do during this stage include;

- Prepare a list of relevant questions to ask. The questions should be based on the project. However, it is impossible to list all likely questions but things like colour scheme, brand objectives, orientation, budget etc.
- Take notes and be very attentive. Repeat questions and be sure the client has a clear picture of what they want. This is to avoid wasted effort due to wrong briefing.
- Don't rush. Allow the client explain before speaking. Do not cut them while they are talking.
- Do not assume you know what they want or what they will like. Ask questions on every detail. Yes, every single detail!
- For each question have samples, you can show them to ensure what they say and what you hear lines up. For instance if they say they love pink, ask them what shade of pink and show them pictures to ensure you are on the same page.
- Assist them in understanding some design terms and nuances if they are not design literate. For instance, they want a combination that is wrong from a design perspective. As an expert, tell them why it will hurt their brand and give suggestions of better options right there.
- Ensure you have the main goal of the project clearly noted, so you can make decisions based on it. Sub goals should be given lesser power in determining the project course

- Show enthusiasm in the discussion and let them know you are excited to be working on the project.
- Assure them you will deliver a professional work.
- Set timelines and ensure both parties agree to it. Rate should have been communicated first before briefing.

2. Brainstorming

This part is where information is processed and ideas are generated. It is very raw and uncontrolled. Some things to do during this stage are:

- Get a sketch pad, draw and write whatever comes to your mind.
- Do research and let ideas flow to you.
- Get ideas by moving around, observing nature, and discussing with people. As you do these, take down notes and sketch ideas on paper.
- Put down as many things as possible. The goal is not to come up with a final design, from multiple options that can be refined and developed further.

The image above is a rough sketch from the idea generation stage of one of my works. I had done this in a meeting that had almost taken me down in boredom. So, you can get ideas anywhere. Always carry a writing material and book with you.

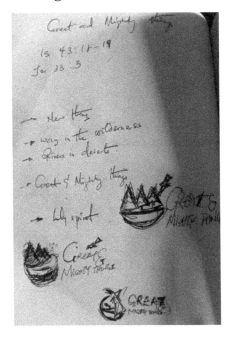

Another set of sketching and brainstorming for a competition. Some people sketch on a device but I prefer to sketch on a white blank page. This was the final product after refining and vector drawing

Keep it flowing, keep it loose and build on it later.

3. Refining/Prototyping

This point is where technical expertise comes into play. Here, your knowledge of software is required to translate your sketch and notes into functional designs. Colour choices will also be worked out, here. Some things to do include;

- Narrow your ideas into the top three or five for some projects i.e. logo design.
- For other projects, you might want to try out different grids and placements to see which one comes out best. Grids are separations in your work that are worked out with lines or shapes like circles. Grids help to make your work well arranged and appear natural.

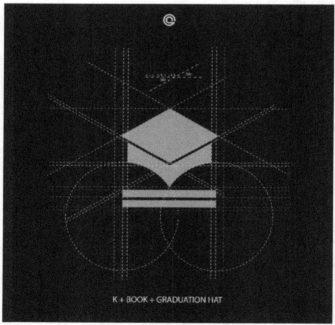

Logo grid for a brand design.
Image Credit: IG@graphicsdaniel

- Try out colour schemes to see that produces the effect you desire best. Mix foreground and background colours and play around with additional colours in your palette.

Finished work after gridding
Image Credit: IG@graphicsdaniel

- Take short breaks to get fresh perspective on fine tuning your selected ideas. This is necessary to make the small tweaks that make all the difference.
- Depending on the project, mix up the orientations and see how the design looks on various applications. This is necessary for a branding project.
- Apply designs on mockups and prepare them for presentation to the client. If there is need for a slide or video presentation, make this and get ready to explain your work.

4. Presentation

This is the moment of truth. As good as a job is, if the client says "No"... then it means it wasn't what they wanted. This stage is critical, and some things to do include;

- Explain the rationale behind the work clearly and give them room to react to what they see.

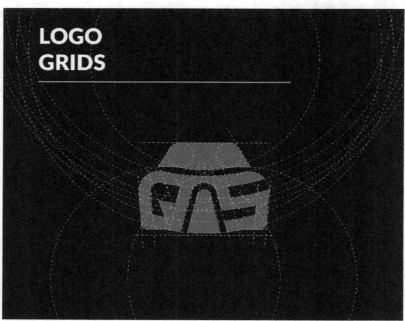

Gridding for a brand mark.
Image Credit: IG@graphicsdaniel

- Take note of any corrections and things they accept.
- Ensure that you are mentally ready to handle the possibility of rejected work.
- For rejected work, there have to be explanations. Let the client say what is off for them, while you listen attentively. This enables you to start from the number 3 step rather than starting over from the number 1 step. Again, make sure dissatisfied client(s) tell you why they rejected the initial work that was delivered.
- Apply diplomacy. I have spoken very well on this under "pricing and dealing with clients"
  Make sure you speak gently and do not try to make your client(s) feel stupid. Also, don't allow them to make you feel stupid or look down on your work. Paying you does not give anyone the license to insult you.

Let them know you are not a machine that auto-produce ideas. Most people turn down work because they have no clear idea as to what they want. Or perhaps, they want too much. Respectfully let them know this.

5. Delivery

If the presentation goes well and the work is accepted, then you will have to send it to the client. Some things to do include;

- Send the files in software format (raw file). Various extensions exist for different programs e.g .psd for Photoshop, .ai for illustrator, .cdr for CorelDraw etc. This is to enable your clients to edit as they please in the future.
- Send the pictures in a way that does not reduce quality. This might involve sending as mail or sending via chat apps as files instead of pictures.

Final Presentation after proper refining.
Image Credit: IG@graphicsdaniel

- Keep a copy of the work with you for your portfolio and future purposes. In case the client misplaces it and needs it again.
- Send a thank you message and ensure your balance is paid before delivery. If there is sufficient level of trust (in the client), then you can collect payment after delivery. The choice is yours.

The path is not always straight from point one to five, but you will always meet these stages in the lifecycle of your project.

What are mockups?

Mockups are templates that transform a graphic work; giving it another look depending on the configuration. Mockups come as PSD (Photoshop documents), AI (Adobe Illustrator) files, and so on. The most popular file format is PSD.

In the hands of a knowledgeable designer, mockups help to give a real-life rendering of certain designs; thus, increasing acceptance and visual appeal. But in the hands of a novice, these mockups can become a stumbling block to learning proper design principles, as they become heavily reliant on them for their design process.

Right ways to use mockups

Mockups are used for presentation. They help the designer show real-life applications of a design to a client, and to facilitate the visual coherence of the work. Let us see a few examples...

Product Packaging

When designing a sticker or product package cover, it natural for you to want your client to see how such a design will look like in real life. And this is where a mockup comes in. Lots of online sites offer free and paid mockups, which are a must-have for any serious designer.

Logo Presentation

A good way to show a client a logo presentation is to use mockups. This does not substitute for a proper 2D logo, but it helps them visualize the application of the logo in real life.

Print Visualizing.

If you plan on printing and you need to see the likely outcomes of your design on print, then mockups are the way. This could include; Signage, flyers, book covers, music tape covers, and the list go on.

Mockups help to give real-life applications to your 2D design, but there are wrong ways to use mockups.

Wrong ways to use mockups

A lot of amateurs rely heavily on mockups to give their design credibility and acceptance, but a savvy client will see through the façade. Here are some ways not to use mockups:

1. As a substitute for learning basic design principles, which we discussed previously.
2. As the focal point of your design. Your 2D design is the focal point as this is what will be used in the branding of the company.
3. As a means to deceive the client into believing they have a functional desirable design job.
4. As the bulk part of your portfolio. Mockups will make up a large part of your portfolio; but your 2D design is what makes people aware that you know your onions.

How to use mockups

Using mockups is pretty easy, and here are the steps to do this:

1. Download a suitable mockup online from sites like mockup world, freepik, etc.
2. Open the mockup with the required software e.g. Photoshop, Illustrator, etc.
3. Locate the visible layer called "Edit me". It is here you are to place your design and delete the original design.
4. Click the "Cancel" icon on the menu bar, and this saves your work rendering. It's based on the mockup specification.
5. Save the image in whatever format you want e.g. Jpg, png, etc.
6. Close the file, when asked whether to save changes click on cancel.

Boom!

After following these steps you should now be able to use mockups effectively. However, if it appears that you still need clarity to crack the nuts associated with the usage of mockups, YouTube videos abound online to help you achieve this. Also, a friend who is knowledgeable in this subject can be of great assistance to you, too. It is quite easy once you get the hang of it.

Design for social media

Image Credit: Google.com

Branding for social media

Social media has become an important tool for business and personal growth. The "audience reach" is endless, and the networking opportunities are overwhelming. Amid this sea of information, it is necessary to know certain tips which when applied by designers and non-designers help their social media pages or accounts have a unique feel. Here are a few tips for more effective social media reach

1. Use a customized color palette: A color palette is basically a combination of colors that are used consistently in your page.

The color palette here is consistent. With the exception of a few posts, this creates high visual coherence

2. Use a selection of fonts: Make sure you pick some fonts. A maximum of three that would pass across the information of your designs. This helps ensure uniformity.

3. Use proper hierarchy in your designs: Make sure your focal points are very clear, and try not to crowd your design with information (through so many letterings). Rather type the

information in the post. The design should draw people to read the post.

The design has very few words but a clear message that encourages the reader to continue on to the text in the post.

4. Use compelling images when possible: You must have heard that a picture is worth a thousand words. This is very true. Therefore, use images as much as possible but be careful to avoid copyright issues. Also try to post high quality images.

This advert utilizes a captivating image of a roaring lion with the clear message "Unleash your brand".

5. Use the right image size: Different social media sites have different image sizes that are optimal. For instance, Facebook and Instagram have a different optimal image size compared to twitter, LinkedIn, Pinterest, etc. So a quick Google search of the social media site's optimal image size(s) will help you create designs that are more effective.

For instance the size for twitter cover photo is a bit different from Facebook.

6. Use templates: Templates are one of the best ways to create highly unique posting structures that are visually appealing. It usually consists of the logo on the proper canvas size, depending on the site, graphic elements, right color pallete, and space for editing information unto. The templates are usually edited to relate new information. Lots of templates should be made to keep the page dynamic.

This is a template for language company so_lingua to post relevant content on their social media page. The size has been optimized for Facebook, Instagram and LinkedIn. It checks all the requirements in number 6.

Using Free Resources

Image Credit: Pexels.com

Free things. Don't we all love them? The world of design is saturated with a lot of free resources that can help take your design to the next level. But first, I have a word of warning regarding the following issues:

Copyright

Intellectual property is guarded by laws that help to protect the owner's interest. A violation of this can result in copyright infringement. Essentially, when you use a photograph, illustration, picture, write up, etc. without seeking permission from the original author this can result in a copyright suit and it is very bad for a brand. Most people do not want to be associated with thieves. When you take and use a person's work without permission, then it is robbery. Unless the authors have given permission expressly for it to be used, ethically it is wrong to do otherwise.

There are tons of resources whose authors have permitted their usage by others. I will give links to some. And of course, if you can afford subscriptions to paid resources it is much better.

Links

1. Fonts: Free fonts are a blessing, a way to give your typography new looks and different feels for free. Creating typeface is a skill that is definitely worth investing time in. I personally have over 10,000 fonts. Not that I use even close to a tenth of it.

www.dafont.com

www.1001fonts.com

www.fonts.com

www.google.com/fonts

2. Stock Images: Unless you have a budget for a photographer then you need stock images. High resolution images abound and help to ease things up for low budget works. Some of these stock image sites are:

www.unsplash.com

www.shutterstock.com

www.freepik.com

www.pexels.com

www.superfamous.com

www.jaymantri.com

www.freedigitalphotos.net

www.pexels.com

3. Mockups: under the chapter on "Using mockups," we talked extensively about mockup usage. Some sites for free mockups are:

www.mockupworld.com

www.freedesignresources.net

www.behance.net

www.freepik.com

www.fribble.com

4. Vectors: Vectors are digital artworks that are defined by lines, curves, shapes etc. Different from bitmap which are defined by pixels

www.freepik.com

www.vecteezy.com

www.vectorstock.com

www.freevector.com

www.psdblast.com

www.graphicburger.com

www.subtlepatterns.com

1. Design Communities: There are many places to get ideas for design work and interact with fellow designers.

www.deviantart.com

www.pinterest.com

www.behance.net

Social media design groups and forums on Instagram, Facebook, twitter etc.

Image Credit: Pexels.com

Setting your rates

Unless you are Santa Claus on a sleigh pulled by fictional reindeer flying across the globe giving free gifts, then you must set rates. Rate is how you intend to charge for your services. It is dependent on your skill level, experience, portfolio strength, and bargaining power. It can be hourly, set by milestones (project steps), or monthly (like a normal salary). It all depends on the way you want it.

No matter how small a project might seem, it is necessary to set appropriate rates. There is no general consensus on how much should be charged but there are some tips to guide you in setting rates;

1. Match your rates to your skill level. If you are still learning, then you cannot command the same rates as an accomplished person in your field.
2. Match your rate to your experience. It is closely related to the first point. The more people you have worked with (or for), the stronger your *commanding power*. Especially if these are well-established brands.
3. Have a means of ensuring you are paid for the job. Many people end up delivering a job and not being paid. In my experience, I once did a job for a friend who refused to pay. It was a bitter but necessary experience. Thus, have a strategy to ensure you collect your money. Some collect a certain percentage before the work starts, and then collect the balance before delivering the final job.
4. Have a uniform rate and actually record it somewhere. This is to avoid giving different rates to different people. Ensure your rates are uniform and do your best to keep it at that.
5. Have a recording system for your income and expenditure. This is very important if you are to know the average amount you spend hourly, and it guides you in setting your rates. If you spend an average of $6 every hour on rent, data, etc. then you have to set a rate that sufficiently covers that amount. There are excellent materials online to guide you in calculating your average expenses.
6. If you freelance for a living, then your rate cannot be joked with. It must be reviewed regularly and communicated to clients.

Bargaining/Negotiating

In the words of John F. Kennedy, "Let us never negotiate out of fear, but let us never fear to negotiate." If there is a word that makes people undercharge, it must be fear. In my work experience, I have realized that a lack of confidence in your ability, what you hope to offer to the client places you at a disadvantage at the negotiating table.

There is a sense of cockiness in what you hope to offer that gives the client a rest of mind. This trust will translate to the right rate payment. Of course, you need to achieve a level of confidence in your work before you can convince a person to pay top money for that service. A track record of delivered work helps your case out a lot. This track record is what is called a portfolio. It is a record of your previous work and how you executed each. A designer must have the skill of negotiating favorable rates, especially when discussing with a person who does not understand the value of your work. Some ways to negotiate better include;

1. Explain clearly the commercial value or implications of your work. Not just the aesthetic side.
2. Grow your portfolio even if it involves doing free work.
3. Become sure of your skill level and do not let anyone talk you down into believing your worth is less.
4. Get positive reviews and refer new clients to them.
5. Keep your old clients happy and they will be your brand marketers.

Free work

A great man once said that you cannot escape the necessary evil of free work. That great man is me and I made that up a long time ago. It is true and every accomplished designer will testify to this. At one point or the other, you will have to do free work. I define free work as work that you collect no rate on, or collect rates that are so little they qualify as mere compensation.

Free work is necessary when starting to build your portfolio. Your family and friends will be the ideal candidates. You will not have the pressure of doing work for a complete stranger, even as it allows you to work with an added freedom of not being paid. And this gives you the flexibility to make mistakes and learn.

In other words, you can approach your friends and family, offering them your services. And when you get gigs from them, execute them with all your energy and tell them to refer people to you. Do not do free work. And even if you will (as a starter trying to build his or her portfolio), don't do it for long. You are not Santa Claus (*lol*!). If a person approaches you to do a job, without the intention to pay for it, kindly refuse. I repeat kindly refuse! Be it, a family member, friend, or a stranger. Reject people who will not value your craft. I will speak more on this later.

As you do free work for a start, begin to charge entry-level rates and rack up more additions to your portfolio. Never use lesser energy and perfection for free work. This free works will be the gateway for the high paying clients you seek.

Meanwhile, you can also create and do works for fictional brands. This is another excellent way of building your portfolio. You should try this if you're a starter. I'll be waiting for your appreciation letter in the long-run.

Diplomacy

If you think diplomacy only applies to governmental relationships, then you need to think again. Diplomacy also involves the skill in dealing with people to avoid or settle hostility.

If you do not know how to talk to people, then your skill might not translate to income (that's more money in your bank account). Hence, the art of discussing with people is as important as becoming proficient in any software usage. Your clients, even though they may be your family members or friends, they have come into a business relationship with you, and therefore the following rules apply:

1. Do not speak rudely no matter how frustrated you are. I once did a logo design for someone (free) and my samples kept being rejected. Even though I felt the business owner didn't have a good eye for design, I replied harshly and she became offended. That relationship was never restored. The bottom line is choosing your words carefully.
2. The customer is not always right. In this line of business, you are to put all the clients choices into consideration, but you must be firm in ensuring they don't push you to deliver terrible

jobs. Some clients do not know solid design principles, and expect you to do whatever they say because they paid. This is something you must say a big "NO" to.

3. Take advice and correction. When a client wants something, make sure you are working along the lines of what they want, and not what you think they should want. Take down corrections to your work without ill feelings and effect them properly. Never get so over confident that you refuse advice or critique on your work.

4. Do not always expect the client to see what you see in the work. That is why you must explain properly, so that the client can appreciate your efforts better. If at the end (after delivering your work to your client), you get a "that's okay" reply, don't get discouraged. People with a solid sense of design will appreciate the work when they see it.

Saying No (Spotting problematic clients)

In your quest to make enough income from your business, you might think that racking up as much clients as possible is the best idea—wrong! I have had some clients I wished I could refund their money and drop the job.

A single unreasonable client can be the source of a bad week, so it is important you spot them and say "No" on time, no matter how attractive their offers might be.

Here are some tips to spot problematic clients;

1. They belittle your work and question your skill. These people question your rates in a derogatory manner with statements like "This is simple, why charge much?"

2. They set unreasonable timelines, and make statements like this: "I need this job tomorrow, rush things up."

3. They have no idea on what they want. When you hear a statement like "Do your thing" please don't. Ask the client what they want, and if they can't give you a concrete answer, wait until they can to avoid wasted effort.

4. They want too many things. A logo with a fish, cross, and three heads. It is absurd what some people want. A lot of times, they even conflict themselves and expect you to do a good job.

Please avoid them or get a very clear picture before you proceed.

5. They want unprofessional work. I have seen clients give the most ridiculous references, and I wonder, "Does this person have no sense of proper design?!"
   Please avoid them, as they will refuse your excellently designed work, in favor of what they term as good design. Let them meet the unprofessional designer to give them what they want.

6. They don't appreciate your work. Greater than money paid is the appreciation of work done. A simple statement like "Thank you", "Great job!", "I am okay with the job", "I love the job "goes along way. And of course, good pat on your back as creative graphic designer. A problematic client stresses you and does not even value your work.

7. Have issues paying. A person who will pay less than the agreed price or delay in payment should be avoided. This is common sense.

Human relationship is complex and you will not have a personal relationship with up to 80% of your clients. So while that project is on, ensure you give the best impression of yourself and/or the company you represent.

PROTECTING YOUR MENTAL HEALTH
FOR CREATIVES

@bluprintdsgns

Image Credit: Unsplash.com

One in four people will be affected by mental or neurological disorders at one point or the other in their lives. I may not present you statistical evidence to support this veracity of this statement, but then it doesn't make it less a fact in our contemporary world.

I have prepared a six-paged carousel (down below) that talks on practical steps to keep your mental health in good shape.

In this line of work, it is particularly easy to suffer from mental illness, especially depression and anxiety attacks. Your health is of paramount importance.
Personally, I have had stretches of anxiety attacks over my work. These anxiety attacks arise from lots of issues; ranging from thinking about how a client(s) will react to my presentation, does my work possess (and reflect) the best quality that my client(s) can ever find, to personal issues. And usually, It affects my appetite, relationship with others, and even gives me stomach upset. This is not the way to go.
A great realization for me, and for anyone who does anything at all, is that, rejection is a part of life. It doesn't mean you are worthless (even if anyone has said that before). Also, rejection doesn't mean you cannot succeed in that field, nor does it mean your work is terrible. Perhaps your skill set is not in line with the client's need, or your presentation is not what the client desires in the work. You shouldn't put yourself in a state of mental disorder; you still have tons of clients who will love your job(s).
I am in no way saying correction shouldn't be taken seriously, neither am I saying your skill shouldn't be improved. Subjectively, I encourage that more than anything. Hone your skills. But the feeling of emptiness and worthlessness at your work and yourself is not the way to go. No matter where you are, remember that every master was once a novice. This is my problem with those who set lofty goals, and hope to achieve them overnight. Do not set yourself up for a colossal heartbreak.
Go through the carousels and take notes, thank me later.

RESIST THE URGE
TO COMPARE

The first thing we do most times when we see a work is to compare it with ours. This is necessary to evaluate our skills but it could also lead to cycles of negative energy overtime. Compare to improve but don't obsess over it.

RESIST THE URGE
TO CRITIQUE

Being a staunch critic is a two edged sword. A judgmental attitude towards the work of others likely means you are never satisfied with your work. Before your point out any mistakes, appreciate the work first.

RESIST THE URGE
TO COMPLICATE

Simplicity is the ultimate sophistication. A tendency to complicate even the simplest concepts is a sure ticket to depression. Most work remain unfinished due to complications that leave the author lost and confused.

RESIST THE URGE
TO CONTROL

It's okay to know that you cannot have total
control over the creative process. Being a
control freak in this line of work is bad for you.
Schedules and deadlines are great. But
inspiration can't be forced.

RESIST THE URGE
TO COMPLAIN

There are a thousand reasons why your work is not how it should be. You keep complaining and sulking about a lack of clients and exposure. Just stop, it is killing your work and killing you. Work with what you have and upgrade as you go on.

RESIST THE URGE
TO CREATE

If you use a machine non-stop without rest, it will break down won't it? You need regular periods off work to relax and refresh. Failure to do this reduces your work quality and has a negative effect on your mental health. Take breaks

RESIST THE URGE
TO CRACK

The urge to give up, quit, abandon a project. It comes in all forms but mental toughness is needed to start and finish a work. Knowing that you put in your best should be good enough for you even if some unreasonable folk talks trash about it.

Note, all images used for the carousels were gotten from pexels.com and unsplash.com.

However, apart from the tips listed here, there are other important things like eating well and exercising. Most creative spend all day behind a computer screen and eat junk. Eat well and stay hydrated, less sugar and carbs. Get good sleep too, if you deprive your brain of rest it will enter overdrive and burn out.

I remember when I was in college and we would read so hard for an exam, some people fell ill before or during the exam. How ironic is that. Your brain is so exhausted you lose your wellbeing when it matters most.

It is also important to stay off drugs and stimulants. Taking hard drugs for inspiration is only a straight ticket to a mental institution at some stage in your life. Too much coffee is bad for you and you know it. I don't take coffee, I just manage my time well, give myself enough room to meet deadlines. How can you deliver if you are dead before the deadline (nice line right?)

Keep your health in good shape and watch the quality of your work improve.

Acknowledgements

My gratitude to God almighty for the success of this book, knows no bounds. Staying motivated to write it, from start to finish, would have been impossible without Him.

Also, my parents have been a pillar that sustaining my focus and striving for the best. I say to them, "Thank you mum and dad. I love you both."

My siblings didn't know on time that I was writing the draft of what turned out as the book you're reading. But since they gained the awareness about it, their support has been overwhelming. I can unapologetically say that, I have got best siblings in the world.

However, my appreciation would not be complete without mentioning my girlfriend. She would always ask for regular updates about my progress. I love you unreservedly.

But how can I forget my uncle, Mr. Cosmos Esekwe, who never hesitated to house me in the course of writing this book. In fact, I wrote a bulk of this book at his place. What a nice place he's got... filled with so much love! Also, I humbly appreciate graphicsdaniel, for granting me permission to use some of his materials in this book.

And finally, I say a big "THANK YOU" to all my teachers, and to you, for reading this book. Without you, all my efforts would have been a beautiful waste of time.

Author's Bio

Esekwe Victor is a professional freelancer with over two years of content creation, graphic design, and consultancy. He is also a teacher, a lover of God, good food, and beautiful art. He lives in Lagos, Nigeria, and does freelance part-time. You can reach him on Facebook @Esekwe Victor, WhatsApp on +2348129677166, Instagram @bluprintdsgns, Twitter @Esekwe Victor.